AF428235

Watch Where You're Going!

Poisonous Animals for Kids

Animal Book 8 Year Old
Children's Animal Books

Be aware and afraid of poisonous animals. Some of them can only live in faraway countries, but some can live nearby. Read further to learn about the **Scorpion, Gold Poison Dart Frog, Black Widow Spider** and the **Colorado River Toad.** These are only a few of the many poisonous animals we should be aware of.

Scorpion in defensive position ready to attack.

Scorpions

What Are Scorpions?

Scorpions are not considered insects, but are in the animal class of arachnids and have eight legs, similar to a spider. They are not all the same, but have similar features. There are more than 1700 species, including the Emperor scorpion and the Arizona Bark scorpion.

What Do Scorpions Look Like?

They have eight legs, similar to all arachnids, however, they have a long tail that has a venomous stinger at the end of it and they also have two large pinchers. Their outer exoskeleton is a hard shell and comes in different colors including green, yellow, blue, brown and black. They also vary in their size. The smallest ones are about one inch long and the larger ones grow up to more than eight inches long.

Scorpion in attack position.

Where Do They Live?

Scorpions can be found just about anywhere, including caves, grasslands, rainforests and deserts. They burrow into the ground in rocks, sand or soil which makes them hard to be spotted by prey and predators.

A dangerous scorpion about to strike.

What Do Scorpions Eat?

They feed mostly on insects, however, the larger ones may eat a small rodent or lizard. When they are hunting, they attack their prey using the claws and paralyze with their stinger on the end of their tail.

Scorpion attacking a millipede.

How Poisonous Are Scorpions?

All species are poisonous. Some of the poisons are specific for a certain type of prey and can be more toxic to various animals. There are approximately 25 species of scorpions that are lethal to humans. You should never try to play with one. If you happen to spot one, you should let your teacher or parents know.

Scorpion protecting itself.

Are They Endangered?

Some are rarer than others, but typically, they are not considered endangered. Some species, such as the Emperor, are protected so as to keep a collector from removing them from their wild habitat.

Golden Poison Arrow Frogs (Phyllobates Terribilis)
in natural rainforest environment.

Golden Poison Dart Frog

The Golden Poison Dart Frog, also known as the Golden Poison Arrow Frog or the Golden Poison Frog, is considered to be an amphibian and its scientific name is *Phyllobates Terribilis*. It is most well-known for its poisonous skin.

Where Does It Live?

This poisonous frog lives close to the coast of the Pacific Ocean in Columbia, South America. The rainforest is its habitat, where the temperature remains warm and rain is abundant. They live in the wild in groups of four to seven since they are social animals.

Golden Poison Dart Frog (Phyllobates terribilis) in natural rainforest environment. Colorful bright yellow tropical frog.

What Does It Eat?

This poisonous frog eats a lot of the same things that other frogs eat; insects like flies, beetles, termites, crickets and ants. Their lengthy tongue allows them to retrieve their food from a distance.

Golden Poison Dart Frog stalking a bug.

How Poisonous Is It?

Its poison is very lethal. It has been reported that it has killed kill humans and one frog has plenty of poison to kill 10 humans. Their poison is an alkaloid poison and the entire of skin of the frog is poisonous, so even touching it can kill. Their poison is so lethal that it can kill a small animal that touches the same paper towel that one of these lethal frogs had just walked on.

The belief is that they get the poison from the insects they eat. If they live in captivity for a period of time, the become less poisonous. The Golden Poison Frog born in captivity is typically harmless.

What Does It Look Like?

They grow to be between one to two inches long. In spite of their name, they are not gold in color. They come in many vibrant colors from orange to yellow to green. The vibrant colors are to ward off predators as the predator will see the vibrant color as something that won't taste good or might be poisonous. This is known as aposematic coloring.

Golden Poison Dart Frog / Phyllobates Terribilis

Are They Endangered?

The Golden Poison Frog is considered to be endangered. While there are many of them in their normal habitat, this habitat is quite small and due to that it is in danger of encroachment by humans.

Golden Poison Dart Frog (Phyllobates Terribilis) in natural rainforest environment.

Black Widow Spider.

The Black
Widow Spider

This lethal spider is known as one of the more dangerous and poisonous spiders located in North America. They are typically known to be black in color and have a red marking located underneath their abdomen, known as the opisthosoma. The red marking is typically shaped similar to an hourglass.

They Are Known As Arachnids

These spiders are not classified as insects. They are considered as Arachnids, which means they are in the class of Arachnida. Unlike insects, that have three body segments, the spiders only have two. They have eight legs.

Black Widow spider.

Their Appearance

The male spider is smaller and lighter than the female. While the female typically appears dark black in color, the male is more than likely going to be dark brown and he does not have the red hourglass marking on his abdomen. The female's body can grow to be about ½ an inch long with a 1 ½ inch leg span. The female is typically twice the size of the male.

Closeup of a black widow spider.

Just How Poisonous Can They Be?

They are the most lethal spider located in North America. The young spiders and the male are typically not considered to be dangerous to us humans. If you get bitten by one of these spiders, immediately get medical attention. If possible, catch it and the spider can then be of assistance in identifying what type of spider it is and how to treat the bite. If you find one of these spiders, do not try to play with it. Let your teacher or parents know immediately.

Closeup black widow spider showing hourglass marking.

Where Can I Find Them?

The female spider will generally build her web close to the ground. When she has found a great spot and proceeds to build her web, she often remains in and around the web most of the time. She will frequently hang upside down in the web to make the red marking easier to spot. This will also warn off predators, once they see its bright color. While eating a spider that is poisonous may not kill the predator, it can make them ill.

Female black widow spider at rest on web.

What Do They Like to Eat?

They are carnivores, which means they eat insects which they can catch in the web, including mosquitoes, beetles, grasshoppers and flies. Occasionally, the female kills and eats the male spider, which is how the name Black Widow came about.

A black widow spider feeding on a grasshopper.

They Can Lay Hundreds of Eggs

The female black widow spider can lay hundreds of eggs at one time. These eggs then remain in a cocoon which has been spun the mother. They have to live on their own once they hatch and only a few survive.

Female black widow spider guarding an egg case.

Colorado River toad (Incilius alvarius), also known as the Sonoran Desert toad.

The Colorado River Toad

This toad is the largest of the toads native to the United States. It is poisonous and no one should handle them, especially children.

Appearance

The Colorado River Toad can grow to be a length of slightly over seven inches. Typically, their skin will be olive green, but can also be a brownish color and their underbelly is white. The skin is leathery and smooth with warts or bumps. They generally have one or two white warts at each corner of their mouth.

The Colorado River toad (Incilius alvarius).

Where Can They Be Found?

They can be found in northern Mexico and the southwest United States. They like the Sonoran Desert which is in California and can also be found in New Mexico and Arizona. They prefer to live in the desert, which is dry and arid. In the summer, they like to burrow into the ground and then will appear at night or when there is rain.

The Colorado River toad (Incilius alvarius), the Sonoran Desert toad, is a psychoactive toad found in northern Mexico and the southwestern United States. Its toxin contains 5-MeO-DMT and bufotenin.

What Do They Eat?

They eat almost anything that will fit in their mouth, such insects, spiders, small frogs and toads, small lizards, beetles and its possible for them to eat a small mouse or other rodent.

Closeup of Colorado River or Sonoran Desert toad (Incilius alvarius) on rock.

Are They Very Poisonous?

The poison it secretes via the glands of its skin is this toad's main defense. While this poison might not kill an adult person, one can become very ill if you touch it and the poison gets into your mouth. Dogs can become ill and even die if they pick one up in their mouth to play with it.

Colorado River or Sonoran Desert toad (Incilius alvarius) relaxing on rock.

Is There a Difference Between a Toad and a Frog?

Toads are typically considered to be a type of frog, so, technically speaking, there is no difference. However, when we refer to toads, we are typically referring to frogs from the family known as bufonidae, which has short legs in the back and stubby bodies. They will generally walk instead of hopping. In addition, they like dryer climates and you will notice a dry warty skin.

Are They Considered to Be Endangered?

Their status is "least concern". However, the toad is "endangered" in California and "threatened" in New Mexico.

Now that you have learned about a few poisonous animals be sure to learn more by going to your local library, researching the internet and ask questions of your teachers, family and friends. And, if you happen to see one of these creatures, do not touch them, and alert your teacher or family!

Visit
BABY PROFESSOR
EDUCATION KIDS
www.BabyProfessorBooks.com
to download Free Baby Professor eBooks
and view our catalog of new and exciting
Children's Books